FOREST BOOKS
PEOPLE ON A BRIDGE

WISŁAWA SZYMBORSKA was born in Bnin in Western Poland in 1923. In 1931 she and her family moved to Kraków. Under German occupation she attended illegal school-classes and during 1945–48 studied Polish Literature and Sociology at the Jagiellonian University in Kraków. During 1953–81 she worked on the Kraków literary weekly *Życie Literackie* as poetry editor and columnist.

Szymborska has published eight volumes of poetry: *Dlatego żyjemy* [That's Why We Are Alive] (1952), *Pytania zadawane sobie* [Questioning Oneself] (1954), *Wołanie do Yeti* [Calling the Yeti] (1957), *Sól* [Salt] (1962), *Sto pociech* [A Hundred Joys] (1967), *Wszelki wypadek* [Chance] (1972), *Wielka liczba* [A Great Number] (1976) and *Ludzie na moście* [People on a Bridge] (1986).

Her poetry has been translated into French, German, Russian, Czech, Hungarian and Dutch, as well as English.

ADAM CZERNIAWSKI is a poet and translator. His most recent collection of poems called **Jesień** [Autumn] was published in Poland in 1989; his translations include the poetry of Kochanowski, Norwid, Staff, Różewicz, Herbert and many others.

PEOPLE
ON
A BRIDGE

Wisława Szymborska

PEOPLE
ON
A BRIDGE

Poems

Introduced and translated
by
ADAM CZERNIAWSKI

FOREST BOOKS
LONDON ☆ 1990 ☆ BOSTON

PUBLISHED BY
FOREST BOOKS

20 Forest View, Chingford, London E4 7 AY, U.K.
61, Lincoln Road, Wayland, MA 01778, U.S.A.

First published 1990

Typeset and printed by Oficyna Cracovia, Poland

British Library Cataloguing in Publication Data
Szymborska, Wisława
    People on a bridge: the poetry of Wisława
    Szymborska.
    I. Title II. Czerniawski, Adam
    891.8517

    ISBN 0-948259-70-1

    Library of Congress Catalogue Card No:
        90-80379

FOREST BOOKS gratefully acknowledge the financial support
of the Arts Council of Great Britain and the support and
encouragement of the Foundation for Polish Culture.

Contents

The particular imagination

The particular imagination

To many people a poet's creative process appears no less interesting than the resulting work. How do poems come about? I don't think there is an account that applies to all poets indiscriminately, and no account can be wholly satisfactory; most are questionable, many unilluminating. But Wisława Szymborska has herself described her own experience: 'If I happen to think in terms of a story, I write a story, if I happen to think in terms of an essay, I write an essay-poem.'* I shall call her account 'conceptualist'. It seems to work like this. The poet has an idea: What was the real reason for Lot's wife looking back? Or: Think of the clandestine pleasures of forbidden free thought in terms of the forbidden fruits of pornography. Or: Imagine our lives as instant, unrehearsed stage performances. In each case the idea is arresting, but also very simple because it can be encapsulated in a sentence like a philosophical proposition. Once an idea like this occurs to the poet, the remaining task is to find appropriately literary clothes for it. Two stages of composition thus appear clearly distinguishable: content, then form. We are in a now somewhat unfamiliar world of pre-Romantic aesthetics, before Coleridge's proclamation of organic form, when it seemed, if required, easy and indeed desirable, to disengage the poem's meaning from its frame without causing serious damage. Since the 19th century this has been thought an impossible task and a disreputable ideal.

---

* Krystyna Nastulanka, **Sami o sobie,** Warsaw 1975, p. 302.

And the poems composed during this period have increasingly underwritten this thesis, from Coleridge's *Kubla Khan* and de Nerval's *El Desdichado,* through Rimbaud's *Illuminations,* Mallarmé's sonnets, on to the surrealists and many others.

In reading such poetry we become aware that the words, both as carriers of meaning, and as sounds and rhythms, contribute subtly to the particular atmosphere and direction of the poems; we become aware that this direction, often wayward and confusing, was being discovered by the poet in the course of composition. Szymborska, on the other hand, gives the impression of knowing exactly where she is going right from the start. The parallel philosophical procedure is to announce a thesis and then to argue for it.

But the distinguished Polish poetry critic Zbigniew Bieńkowski cautioned against any claim that there might be even a suspicion of a philosophical, rational, element in Szymborska's poetry: '...this poetry with its wise naiveté or naive wisdom, which is precisely a poetry open to a world of thought, is a poetry which is most profoundly anti-intellectual. Szymborska neither feels nor thinks in terms of schemas, she employs no categories, she does not prove or disprove theses or sophistries; she has the courage, more, she is lucky to have the ability to think in her own way, she has the courage and the luck to indulge in homely, amateur thought. She is always herself.'**

One can appreciate Bieńkowski's nervousness. The notion of intellectualist, conceptualist poetry brings to mind dry, neo-classical academicism, so unlike the witty, sceptical or bemused bravura poetic performances which have earned Szymborska immense popularity, as well as prestige. But the fact that many intellects with literary ambitions have failed to give poetic shape to their inventions, is no proof that the rational is inimical to the poetic, or that the philosophy of a poet, if it is to succeed, has to be a set of naive home-spun musings. Bieńkowski's *caveats* date back to 1973, since when

---

** Zbigniew Bieńkowski, *Poetyckie znaki zodiaku: Szymborska,* **Poezja,** March 1973, Warsaw, p. 97.

Szymborska's conceits have become, if anything, more sophisticated, more intellectual. In fact, the poems in **Section III** could, like **Alice in Wonderland** or Borges' fables, serve as opening gambits in a philosophical or scientific debate. How real is reality (**Reality:** *'a riddle | that's insoluble'*); are we alone in the universe (**Unwritten poem reviewed**); what is the nature of our existence (**A version of events**); can we arrest the flow of time (**People on a bridge**); is there a mind inside a body (**Experiment**); are we evolutionally better adapted than creatures now extinct (**A dinosaur's skeleton**); is there life after death (**Elegiac account**)?

When we see these poems thus reduced to simply stated, yet profound epistemological questions, we wonder whether such artefacts could possibly have housed a poetic spirit. It is a measure of Szymborska's skill that she can rise to these challenges with remarkable success.

Yet Szymborska herself, when she asserts in **Big numbers** that her imagination *'doesn't cope well with big numbers'* and is *'still moved by singularity'*, appears to acknowledge Bieńkowski's worries. For 'intellectual' signifies a concern with universals, perhaps it *is* the universal, which is the province of philosophy rather than poetry. But the distinction isn't that simple. There are ways of being general (and of being particular), some of which take us into philosophy, some of which add a philosophical dimension to what is crucially poetic. When Szymborska writes **In praise of my sister**, she is undoubtedly being particular, even autobiographical, for we happen to know that she has a sister. But can she be particular about the number *pi*? Numbers are quintessentially general and *pi* additionally has the no less philosophically interesting property of running on for ever. Any endeavour to endow this concept with particularity is surely doomed to failure. Yet there is no doubt that Szymborska's treatment of *pi* is poetic. One test lies in the answer to the question: would a philosopher or a mathematician treat *pi* the way Szymborska has done? Clearly not. But unfortunately that in itself is no proof that the poet's treatment of this subject is necessarily poetic: it may be merely perverse, whimsical or just plain dull. Proof is not available in aesthetic judgments, but if wit, imagination and a sense of style and form are important ingredients of good poetry, then **Pi** is a good poem. Szymborska's other 'philosophical' poems need to be considered in a similar way.

Szymborska belongs to the same generation as Różewicz and Herbert, the two poets who are already quite familiar to English readers. The three were born within four years of each other. They have several characteristics in common and it is, I think, interesting and instructive to glance at the similarities and the differences. For instance, both rely heavily on cultural references: Szymborska will take up the concept of the Babel-like confusion of tongues to create an intimate dialogue between estranged lovers, while Herbert will use **Hamlet** as a spring-board for a brisk political manifesto by Fortinbras. Both Szymborska and Herbert are likely to find inspiration in a painting, but while Szymborska will in **People on a Bridge** reflect coolly upon humanity's obsession with time, Herbert will in **The Passion of Our Lord painted by an anonymous hand from the circle of Rhenish Masters** focus on the more palpable question of suffering. Szymborska's rationalist scientific turn of mind enables her to view humanity from a distance, the way humans might observe the antics of ants. This is never Herbert's perspective, for the disciplines which underpin his poetry (history, religion, art) root him more securely in the human predicament. Perhaps it is in the sphere of politics that Szymborska and Herbert come closest: one thinks of her **Utopia** and his **Pan Cogito: the return.**

Herbert, even when he puts on the mask of Pan Cogito or Fortinbras or a Roman pro-consul, always employs the same voice, carefully measured, urbane, wearily ironic, yet easily flowing but never demotic or vulgar. Szymborska, on the other hand, is more Browningian. There are marked differences between the voice that nervously narrates a terrorist's activity (**The terrorist, he watches**), and the one that addresses a learned gathering (**A dinosaur's skeleton**) and there is a range of intonations and rhythms in the various voices in **On the tower of Babel** and **Funeral.**

One undoubtedly shared feature is this ability to capture a vast range of themes in seemingly relaxed, yet always exacting, speech patterns. And here they both owe a debt to Różewicz, who was responsible, in the late forties, for loosening up and 'reducing' poetic language, stripping it of fancy ornamentations.

This stylistic affinity may tempt us to look for further similarities in all three poets, but a strong dividing line meets us when we return to the notion of conceptualist poetry. Różewicz's poems never display a clear distinction between concept and execution, partly or mainly, no doubt, because Różewicz does not pursue a conceit with the same relentless logic that Szymborska or Herbert does. His poems twist and turn unexpectedly, plunge into darkness and mystery. Szymborska, like Herbert, is a daylight poet; in the interview already quoted she declared forcibly: 'I would like everything I write to be clear, intelligible, and I worry a lot if something proves incomprehensible to a reader.'*** Their poems radiate a facility and elegance, they maintain a certain — classical, one is tempted to say — equilibrium and balance, even when they deal with human tragedy and metaphysical horror.

These reflections may frighten the reader into concluding, despite Szymborska's protestations, that her poems require immense intellectual effort and may be totally incomprehensible, at least at first reading. Nothing could be further from the truth: her poems immediately seduce us with their spontaneity and openness. As she herself says, seemingly apologetically, in the oft-quoted lines from **Beneath one little star:**

Speech — don't blame me for borrowing big words
and then struggling to make them light.

*** *Op.cit.*, p. 305.

Adam Czerniawski

Translator's note

A portion of these translations had first appeared in my anthology **THE BURNING FOREST** (Bloodaxe Books, 1988); a few have undergone very minor revisions. The remaining translations have been prepared specifically for this edition. I have relied on texts in **Wszelki wypadek, Wielka liczba, Poezje wybrane (II)** and **Ludzie na moście**; translations of recent uncollected poems are based on texts published in **Twórczość** (Warsaw), **Odra** (Wrocław) and **Puls** (London).

The bulk of the work was completed in the infinitely hospitable and tranquil household of Jaga and Bogdan Czaykowski in Vancouver during September–October 1989.

Richard Edgcumbe has helped me locate the Hiroshige Utagawa print which inspired Wisława Szymborska's title poem. Ann, Fiona and Stefan Czerniawski have cast a critical eye over the manuscript.

A.Cz.

The poems

Ludzie na moście

Dziwna planeta i dziwni na niej ci ludzie.
Ulegają czasowi, ale nie chcą go uznać.
Mają sposoby, żeby swój sprzeciw wyrazić.
Robią obrazki jak na przykład ten:

Nic szczególnego na pierwszy rzut oka.
Widać wodę.
Widać jeden z jej brzegów.
Widać czółno mozolnie płynące pod prąd.
Widać nad wodą most i widać ludzi na moście.
Ludzie wyraźnie przyspieszają kroku,
bo właśnie z ciemnej chmury
zaczął deszcz ostro zacinać.

Cała rzecz w tym, że nic nie dzieje się dalej.
Chmura nie zmienia barwy ani kształtu.
Deszcz ani się nie wzmaga, ani nie ustaje.
Czółno płynie bez ruchu.
Ludzie na moście biegną
ściśle tam, co przed chwilą.

Trudno tu obejść się bez komentarza:
To nie jest wcale obrazek niewinny.
Zatrzymano tu czas.
Przestano liczyć się z prawami jego.
Pozbawiono go wpływu na rozwój wypadków.
Zlekceważono go i znieważono.

Za sprawą buntownika,
jakiegoś Hiroshige Utagawy,
(istoty, która zresztą
dawno i jak należy minęła),
czas potknął się i upadł.

People on a bridge

A strange planet with its strange people.
They yield to time but don't recognise it.
They have ways of expressing their protest.
They make pictures, like this one for instance:

At first glance, nothing special.
You see water.
You see a shore.
You see a boat sailing laboriously upstream.
You see a bridge over the water and people on the bridge.
The people are visibly quickening their step,
because a downpour has just started
lashing sharply from a dark cloud.

The point is that nothing happens next.
The cloud doesn't change its colour or shape.
The rain neither intensifies nor stops.
The boat sails on motionless.
The people on the bridge
run just where they were a moment ago.
It's difficult to avoid remarking here:
this isn't by any means an innocent picture.
Here time has been stopped.
Its laws have been ignored.
It's been denied influence on developing events.
It's been insulted and spurned.

Thanks to a rebel,
a certain Hiroshige Utagawa
(a being which as it happens
has long since and quite properly passed away)
time stumbled and fell.

Może to tylko psota bez znaczenia,
wybryk na skalę paru zaledwie galaktyk,
na wszelki jednak wypadek
dodajmy, co następuje:

Bywa tu w dobrym tonie
wysoko sobie cenić ten obrazek,
zachwycać się nim i wzruszać od pokoleń.

Są tacy, którym i to nie wystarcza.
Słyszą nawet szum deszczu,
czują chłód kropel na karkach i plecach,
patrzą na most i ludzi,
jakby widzieli tam siebie,
w tym samym biegu nigdy nie dobiegającym
drogą bez końca, wiecznie do odbycia
i wierzą w swoim zuchwalstwie,
że tak jest rzeczywiście.

Maybe this was a whim of no significance,
a freak covering just a pair of galaxies,
but we should perhaps add the following:

Here it's considered proper
to regard this little picture highly,
admire it and thrill to it from age to age.

For some this isn't enough.
They even hear the pouring rain,
they feel the cool drops on necks and shoulders,
they look at the bridge and the people
as if they saw themselves there
in the self-same never-finished run
along an endless road eternally to be travelled
and believe in their impudence
that things are really thus.

Wislawa Szymborska

I

Big numbers

Four billion people on this earth,
but my imagination is as it was.
It doesn't cope well with big numbers.
It's still moved by singularity.
It flies in the dark like a beam or a torch,
which reveals only the nearest faces,
while the rest are condemned to oversight,
un-regret, non-thought.
But even Dante couldn't have stemmed this rush.
And what if one even isn't him.
And even if all the Muses came.

Non omnis moriar — it's too early to fret.
But do I wholly live and is that enough.
It never was, and especially now.
Rejecting I choose, there's no other way,
but what I do reject more numerous is,
and denser and more than ever insistent.
At the price of indescribable losses — a few verses, a sigh.
To a rousing call I respond in whispers.
What I pass over in silence I will not express.
A mouse at the foot of the maternal mountain.
Life lasts a few signs clawed in sand.

My dreams — even they are not, as they ought to be,
                                                    populous.
They have more solitariness than tumults and crowds.
Occasionally someone long-dead drops in for a moment.
A single hand turns the door-knob.
The empty house is overgrown with echo's extensions.
From its steps I run down into a peaceful
valley, apparently unclaimed, already out-of-date.

But whence this space in me still —
I have no idea.

Beneath one little star

My apologies to the accidental for calling it necessary.
However, apologies to necessity if I happen to be wrong.
Hope happiness won't be angry if I claim it as my own.
May the dead forget they barely smoulder in my
                                        remembrance.
Apologies to time for the abundance of the world missed
                                        every second.
Apologies to my old love for treating the new as the first.
Forgive me, distant wars, for bringing flowers home.
Forgive me, open wounds, that I prick my finger.
Apologies to those calling from the abyss for a record of a
                                        minuet.
Apologies to people catching trains for sleeping at dawn.
Pardon me, baited hope, for my sporadic laugh.
Pardon me, deserts, for not rushing with a spoon-ful of
                                        water;
and you too, hawk, unchanged in years, in that self-same
                                        cage,
staring motionless, always at the self-same spot,
forgive me, even if you are stuffed.
Apologies to the hewn tree for the four table-legs.
Apologies to the big questions for small replies.
Truth, don't pay me too much attention.
Seriousness — be magnanimous.
Mystery of Being — suffer me to pluck threads from your
                                        train.
Soul — don't blame me for having you but rarely.
Apologies to everyone for failing to be every him or her.
I know that while I live nothing can excuse me,
since I am my own impediment.
Speech — don't blame me for borrowing big words
and then struggling to make them light.

In praise of my sister

My sister doesn't write poems,
and I don't think she'll suddenly start writing poems.
She is like her mother who didn't write poems,
and like her father, who didn't write poems either.
Under my sister's roof I feel safe:
my sister's husband would rather die than write poems.
And — this begins to sound like a found poem —
none of my relations is engaged in writing poems.

There are no old poems in my sister's files
and there aren't any new ones in her handbag.
And when my sister invites me to lunch,
I know she has no plans to read me her poems.
Her soups are excellently improvised,
there is no coffee spilt on her manuscripts.

There are many families where no one writes poems,
but where they do — it's rarely just one person.
Sometimes poetry splashes down in cascades of generations,
creating terrible whirlpools in mutual feelings.

My sister cultivates a quite good spoken prose
and her writing's restricted to holiday postcards,
the text promising the same each year:
that when she returns
she'll tell us
all
all
all about it.

Portrait of woman

Must present alternatives.
Change, but on condition that nothing changes.
That is easy, impossible, difficult, worth trying.
Her eyes are, as required, now deep blue, now grey,
black, sparkling, unaccountably filled with tears.
She sleeps with him as one of many, as the one and only.
She'll bear him four children, no children, one.
Naive, but gives best advice.
Weak, but she'll carry.
She has no head, so she'll have a head,
reads Jaspers and women's magazines.
Has no clue what that nut is for and will build a bridge.
Young, young as usual, always still young.
Holds in her hands a sprarrow with a broken wing,
her own money for a long and distant journey,
a chopper, a poultice and a glass of vodka.
Where is she running, perhaps she's tired.
But no, only a little, very, it's no matter.
She either loves him or she's just stubborn.
For better, for worse and for love of God.

Lot's wife

I looked back supposedly curious.
But besides curiosity I might have had other reasons.
I looked back regretting the silver dish.
Through carelessness — tying a sandal strap.
In order not to keep staring at the rigthteous nape
of my husband, Lot.
Because of sudden conviction that had I died
he wouldn't have stopped.
Being humble yet disobedient.
Listening for pursuers.
Touched with silence, hoping God had changed His mind.
Our two daughters were already disappearing beyond the
                                                    hilltop.

I felt my age. Distance,
futility of wandering. Drowsiness.
I looked back when setting down the bundle.
I looked back in terror where to step next.
My path suddenly teeming with snakes,
spiders, field mice and baby vultures.
Now neither good nor evil — just everything living
crawled and hopped in crowded panic.
I looked back in desolation.
Ashamed of running away in stealth.
Wanting to scream, to turn back.
Or only when a gust of wind
untied my hair and lifted up my skirts.

I had a feeling they were watching from the walls of Sodom
with bursts of hearty laughter again and again.
I looked back in anger.
To savour their perdition.
I looked back willessly.
It was only a rock slipping, growling beneath me.
It was a crevice suddenly cut my way off.
A hamster trotted on the edge on two paws
and then it was we both looked back.

No, no. I ran on,
I crawled and I soared
until darkness crashed from heaven
and with it hot gravel and dead birds.
Losing breath I often swerved.
If anyone saw me, would have thought I was dancing.
Conceivably, my eyes were open.

Homecoming

He was back. Said nothing.
But it was clear something had upset him.
He lay down in his suit.
Hid his head under the blanket.
Drew up his knees.
He's about forty, but not at this moment.
He exists — but only as much as in his mother's belly
behind seven skins, in protective darkness.
Tomorrow he is lecturing on homeostasis
in metagalactic space travel.
But now he's curled up and fallen asleep.

Laughter

The little girl I used to be —
I know her, of course.
I have some photographs
of her brief life.
I feel an amused pity
for the handful of verses she wrote.
I recall an incident or two.

But
to make the one who is here with me
laugh and embrace me,
I will relate just one little story:
the adolescent crush
of that ugly duckling.

I tell him
she was in love with a student,
that is, hoped
he would look at her.

I tell him
how I ran towards him
with a bandage on my woundless head
so that, Oh! he would at least ask
what the matter is.

A funny little thing.
How was she to know
that even despair brings rewards
if you're lucky
to live longer.

I would have given her money to buy a bun.
To go to the pictures.
Go away, I'm busy.

Can't you see
the light's off.
Don't you understand
the door is closed.
Stop rattling the handle —
he who is laughing,
he who's embracing me,
he is not your student.

Best for you to return
whence you came.
I owe you nothing,
I'm an ordinary woman
who only knows
when
to betray someone's secret.

Don't stare at us
with those eyes of yours
too widely open
like the eyes of the dead.

On the tower of Babel

What time is it? — Yes, I'm happy
and all I need is a bell round my neck
to tinkle over you when you sleep.
— *Didn't you hear the storm, then? The wind shook the walls,
the tower like a lion yawned with its huge gate
on a groaning hinge.* — Don't you remember?
I wore a plain dark dress
clasped over the shoulder. — *And immediately
the sky splintered in manifold blasts.* — How could I have
entered,

you weren't alone. *Suddenly I saw
colours that predated sight.* — Pity
you can't promise. — *You're right,
must have been a dream.* — Why do you lie,
why do you call me by her name,
do you love her still? — *Oh yes, I'd like you
to stay with me.* — I'm not bitter,
I should have guessed.
— *You keep thinking of him?* — But I'm not crying.
— *And is that all?* — No one but you.
— *At least you're honest* — Don't worry,
I'll be leaving town. — *Don't worry,
I'll go away.* — Your hands so beautiful.
— *That's an old story, the blade cut through
but left the bones intact.* — No need to,
really, my dear, no need. — *I have no idea
of the time, and I don't wish to have.*

Happy love

Happy love. Is that normal,
is that serious, is that useful —
what does the world get out of two people
who don't see the world?

Lifted towards each other for no valid reason,
no different from a million others, but convinced
that it had to be thus — as reward for what? Nothing;
light falling from nowhere —
why on them and not on others?
Does this offend justice? Yes.
Does it upset solicitously piled principles,
does it upset morals? It does upset and topple them.

Look at these happy ones:
would they at least put on some disguise,
pretend a despondency to sustain their friends!
Hear how they laugh — offensively.
The language they use — seemingly intelligible.
As for those ceremonies, the fuss,
their fanciful reciprocal duties —
they look like a conspiracy behind humanity's back!

It's hard to predict the outcome
if their example could be followed.
What would sustain religions and poets,
what would be remembered, what abandoned,
who would wish to stay within its bounds.
Happy love. Is it necessary?
It's tactful and sensible to ignore this scandal in Life's higher
                                                              spheres.
Fine babies are born without its assistance.
Never, never could it populate the earth,
given its rare occurrence.

Let people who haven't known happy love
insist it's nowhere to be found.

With such faith it'll be easier for them to live and to die.

Thank-you

I owe a lot
to those I don't love.

Relieved to acknowledge
they are closer to someone else.

Joy at not being
the wolf of their sheep.

With them I am at peace,
with them I'm free,
and this love can neither give
nor knows how to take.

I don't wait for them
from window to door.
Patient
almost like a sundial
I understand
what love does not,
and forgive
what love would never have forgiven.

Between a meeting and a letter
it's not an eternity that passes,
but simply a few days or weeks.
Travels with them are always a success,
concerts heard through,
cathedrals toured,
landscapes distinct.

And when seven hills and rivers
divide us,
these are hills and rivers
we know well from maps.

It's their own achievement
if they live in three dimensions,
in nonlyrical and unrhetorical space,
with a real, that is, a mobile horizon.

They themselves don't know
how much they carry empty-handed.

"I owe them nothing"
love would have commented
on this open subject.

An old singer

"He now sings: *trala tra la.*
But I used to sing: *trala tra la.*
Can you hear the difference?
And instead of standing here, he stood here
and looked there, not there,
though it was from over there, and not from over there
that she used to run in, not like now *pampa rampa pam,*
but just simply *pampa rampa pam,*
the unforgettable Tschubeck-Bombonieri,
but who
remembers her now —"

Wrong number

A telephone's been ringing in a gallery room
at midnight when there's no one there;
had there been someone sleeping, he'd now be aware,
but here are only sleepless bards of doom,
holding their breath and with a vacant look,
while the seemingly lively wife of a crook
stares fixedly at that ringing box,
but no, no, she doesn't move her arm,
she's caught, mutely passive, like the rest
who inattentively ignore the alarm,
displaying, I swear it, greater black humour
than if the chamberlain himself had left the frame
(though nothing save silence rings in his ears).
And as regards the fact that someone in town
is naively not putting the receiver down,
having dialled wrongly — he lives and therefore errs.

Perfect

— *Thou art perfect, then, our ship hath touch'd upon*
The deserts of Bohemia? Aye, my lord.
That's from Shakespeare, who, I'm perfect,
was not someone else. Some facts, a date,
a portrait near contemporary... Not enough? Should one
                                                    await
the proof already snatched up by the Great Sea and hurled
upon Bohemian beaches of this world?

Π

Π deserves our full admiration
three point one four one.
All its following digits are also non-recurring,
five nine two because it never ends.
It cannot be grasped *six five three five* at a glance,
eight nine in a calculus
seven nine in imagination,
or even *three two three eight* in a conceit, that is, a
                                        comparison
four six with anything else
two six four three in the world.
The longest snake on earth breaks off after several metres.
Likewise, though at greater length, do fabled snakes.
The series comprising Π
doesn't stop at the edge of the sheet,
it can stretch across the table, through the air,
through the wall, leaf, bird's nest, clouds, straight to heaven,
through all the heavens' chasms and distensions.
How short, how mouse-like, is the comet's tail!
How frail a star's ray, that it bends in any bit of space!
Meanwhile, *two three fifteen three hundred nineteen*
my telephone number the size of your shirt
the year nineteen hundred and seventy three sixth floor
the number of inhabitants sixty-five pennies
the waist measurement two fingers a charade a code,
in which *singing still dost soar, and soaring ever singest*
and *please be cálm*
and also *heaven and earth shall pass away,*
but not Π, no, certainly not,
she's still on with her passable *five*
above-average *eight*
the not-final *seven*
urging, yes, urging a sluggish eternity
to persevere.

II

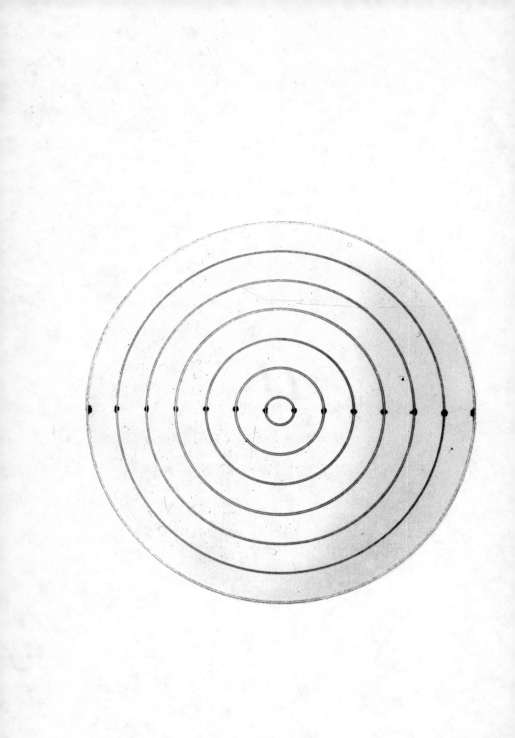

The terrorist, he watches

The bomb will explode in the bar at twenty past one.
Now it's only sixteen minutes past.
Some will still have time to enter,
some to leave.

The terrorist's already on the other side.
That distance protects him from all harm
and, well, it's like the pictures:

A woman in a yellow jacket, she enters.
A man in dark glasses, he leaves.
Boys in jeans, they're talking.
Sixteen minutes past and four seconds.
The smaller one, he's lucky, mounts his scooter,
but that taller chap, he walks in.

Seventeen minutes and forty seconds.
A girl, she walks by, a green ribbon in her hair.
But that bus suddenly hides her.
Eighteen minutes past.
The girl's disappeared.
Was she stupid enough to go in, or wasn't she.
We shall see when they bring out the bodies.

Nineteen minutes past.
No one else appears to be going in.
On the other hand, a fat bald man leaves.
But seems to search his pockets and
at ten seconds to twenty past one
he returns to look for his wretched gloves.

It's twenty past one.
Time, how it drags.
Surely, it's now.
No, not quite.
Yes, now.
The bomb, it explodes.

A contribution on pornography

There is no debauchery worse than thought.
This wantonness is rampant like a wind-blown weed
on a bed reserved for begonias.

For those who think, nothing is sacred.
Brazenly calling everything by name,
perverse analyses, meretricious syntheses,
wild and dissolute pursuit of naked facts,
lustful petting of sensitive subjects,
a spawning ground of opinions — that's just what they're
after.
On a clear day, under cover of darkness,
they consort in pairs, triangles and rings.
No constraint on age or sex of partners.
Friends corrupt friends.
Degenerate daughters deprave their fathers.
Their eyes gleam, their cheeks glow.
A brother pimps for his younger sister.

They prefer the fruit
of the forbidden tree of knowledge
to pink boobs in illustrated mags —
that essentially simple-minded pornography.
The books that divert them have no pictures,
their sole pleasure are special sentences
scored with thumbnail or crayon.

In what shocking positions
with what licentious simplicity
mind can impregnate mind!
Positions unknown even to the Kama Sutra.
During these trysts only tea is steaming.
People sit on chairs, move their lips.
Each crosses his own legs.
So one foot touches the floor,
the other swings free.
But occasionally someone gets up,
goes to the window
and through a chink in the curtains
watches the street.

Funeral

— so suddenly, who could have guessed
— nerves, and cigarettes, I did warn him
— passably, thank you
— unwrap those flowers
— in his brother's case it was the heart, must be in the
                                                                         family
— I would never recognise you with that beard
— only himself to blame, always mixed up in something
— that new one was to speak, can't see him
— Kazek's in Warsaw, Tadek's abroad
— only you were clever enough to take an umbrella
— he was the ablest — doesn't matter now
— it's a connecting room, Basia won't agree
— yes, he was right, but that's no excuse
— door varnishing included — guess how much
— two yolks, a spoonful of sugar
— not his business, shouldn't have meddled
— only in blue and only in small sizes
— five times and never any answer
— all right, I could have, and so could you
— at least she held down that little job
— no idea, probably relatives
— the priest's quite a Belmondo
— I've never been in this part of the cemetery
— I dreamt about him last week, had a premonition
— the daughter is quite pretty
— we're all in the same boat
— condolences to the widow, must rush
— but is used to sound more dignified in Latin
— it's all in the past now
— goodbye, Marta
— let's find a beer somewhere
— give me a ring, we'll talk
— catch a 4 or a 12
— I go this way
— we go over there

33

A dinosaur's skeleton

Beloved Brothers,
we see here an instance of bad proportions:
the dinosaur's skeleton soars before us —

Dear Friends,
to the left, a tail into one infinity,
to the right, a neck into another —

Worthy Comrades,
in the middle, four paws stuck in the slime
beneath a heap
of a carcass —

Gracious Citizens,
nature makes no mistakes, but she delights in pranks:
do please notice that funny little head —

Ladies and Gentlemen,
this little head could forsee nothing
and therefore belongs to an extinct reptile —

Respected Assembly,
too little brain, too great an appetite,
more silly sleep than wise fear —

Honourable Guests,
in this respect we're in much better shape,
life is beautiful and the earth is ours —

Distinguished Delegates,
the starry heavens above the thinking reed,
the moral law within it —

Excellent Commission,
it's succeeded once
and perhaps only beneath this sun —

Ruling Council,
what nimble hands,
what eloquent lips,
how much head on the shoulders —

Supreme Authority,
what responsibility in place of a tail —

Experiment

In a short before the feature film,
in which actors did all they could
to move me and make me laugh,
they screened an interesting experiment
with a head.

A moment earlier
the head still belonged to***,
was now cut off,
we all could see it had no body.
Tubes of an apparatus dangled from its nape,
ensuring a supply of blood.
The head
was well.

Expressing no pain or even surprise,
its eyes followed a moving torch;
cocked its head when a bell rang.
With its moist nose it could distinguish
the smell of bacon from odourless non-being
and licked itself with obvious relish,
it salivated respect for physiology.

A faithful doggy head,
a decent doggy head,
when stroked, it narrowed its eyes
convinced it still is part of a whole
which relaxed its back when petted
and wagged its tail.
I thought about happiness and felt fear.
For if that were all life was about,
the head
was happy.

Utopia

An island where everything becomes clear.

Here one can stand on the ground of proofs.

The only road has its destination.

Shrubs are burdened with answers.

Here grows the free of Proper Conjecture,
its branches eternally untangled.

The dazzlingly straight tree of Understanding
is next to a spring called Ah So That's How It Is.

The deeper you're in the wood, the wider grows
the Valley of Obviousness.

Whatever the doubt, the wind blows it away.

Echo speaks uncalled
and readily solves the mysteries of worlds.

On the right a cave where sense reclines.

On the left a lake of Deep Conviction.

Truth stirs from the bottom and lightly breaks the surface.

Unshakeable Certainty dominates the vale
and Essence of Things spreads from its head.

Despite these attractions, the island is deserted,
and the tiny footmarks seen along the shores
all point towards the sea.

As though people always went away from here
and irreversibly plunged into the deep.

In life that's inconceivable.

III

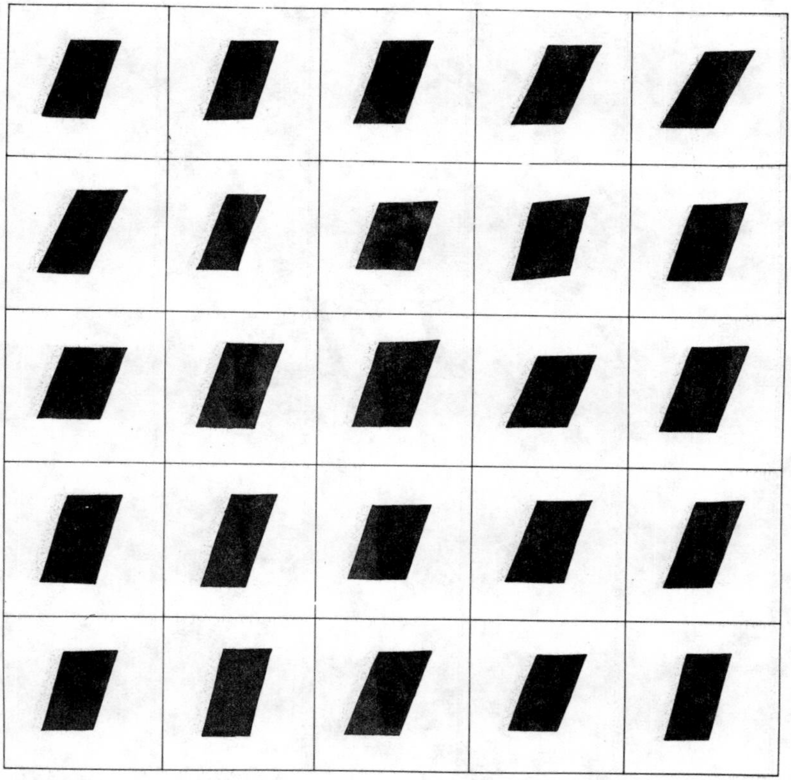

Reality

Reality doesn't vanish
the way dreams do.
No rustle, no bell
disperses it,
no cry or thump
rouses from it.

Images in dreams
are blurred and uncertain,
open to many
interpretations.
Reality denotes reality,
and that's a greater puzzle.

Dreams have keys.
Reality opens on itself
and won't quite shut.
It trails
school reports and stars,
it drops butterflies
and the souls* of old irons,
headless hats
and shards of clouds
resulting in a riddle
that's insoluble.
Without us there would be no dreams.
The one, without whom there would be no reality,
is unknown
while the product of his sleeplessness
affects everyone
that wakes.

---

* The hot metal bar that used to be inserted into old non-electric irons is called 'soul' in Polish. (*Transl.*)

41

It's not dreams that are mad,
reality is mad,
if only because of the tenacity
with which it clings
to the course of events.

In dreams our recently dead
still survives,
he even enjoys good health
and recovered youth.
Reality displays
his dead body.
Reality retreats not an inch.

The volatility of dreams
allows memory to shake them off.
Reality needn't fear being forgotten.
It's a tough nut.
It sits on our shoulders,
lies heavily on our hearts,
bars the way.
There is no escape from her,
she accompanies each flight.
There is no stop
on the route of our journey
where she isn't waiting.

Miracle mart

Common miracle:
the happening of many common miracles.

Ordinary miracle:
invisible dogs barking
in the silence of the night.

A miracle among many:
a tiny ethereal cloud
able to cover a large heavy moon.

Several miracles in one:
an alder reflected in water
moreover turned from left to right
moreover growing crown downwards
yet not reaching the bottom
though the waters are shallow.

An everyday miracle:
soft gentle breezes
gusting during storms.

Any old miracle:
cows are cows.

And another like it:
just this particular orchard
from just this pip.

Miracle without frock coat or top hat:
a scattering of white doves.

Miracle — what else would you call it:
today the sun rose at 3.14
and will set at 20.01.

Miracle which doesn't sufficiently amaze:
though the hand has fewer than six fingers
yet it has more than four.

Miracle — just look around:
the world ever-present.

An extra miracle, just as everything is extra:
what is unthinkable
is thinkable.

In praise of dreams

In my dream
I paint like Vermeer of Delft.

I speak fluent Greek
and not just with the living.

I drive a car
which obeys me.

I am gifted,
I compose epic verse.

I hear voices
as clearly as genuine saints.

My piano performances
would simply amaze you.

I fly the way prescribed,
that is, out of myself.

Falling off a roof
I know how to land softly on the lawn.

Breathing under water
is no problem.

I'm not complaining:
I managed to discover Atlantis.

It's a pleasure always
to wake before death.

Immediately war starts
I turn over to a better side.

I exist, but don't have to be
a child of the times.

Some years ago
I saw two suns.

And the day before yesterday a penguin.
As clearly as this.

Instant living

Instant living.
Unrehearsed performance.
Untried-on body.
A thoughtless head.

I am ignorant of the role I perform.
All I know is it's mine, can't be exchanged.

What the play is about
I must guess promptly on stage.

Poorly prepared for the honour of living
I find the imposed speed of action hard to bear.
I improvise though I loathe improvising.
At each step I trip over my ignorance.
My way of life smacks of the provincial.
My instincts are amateurish.
The stage-fright that is my excuse only humiliates me more.
Mitigating circumstances strike me as cruel.

Words and gestures that cannot be retracted,
stars not counted to the end,
my character like a coat I button up running —
this is the sorry outcome of such haste.

If only one could practice ahead at least one Wednesday,
repeat a Thursday!
But now Friday's already approaching with a script I don't
                                                        know.

Is this right? — I ask
(in a rasping voice,
since they didn't even let me clear my throat in the wings).

You're deluded if you think it's only a simple exam
set in a makeshift office. No.
I stand among the stage-sets and see they're solid.
I am struck by the precision of all the props.
The revolving stage's been turning for quite some time.
Even the furthest nebulae are switched on.
Oh, I have no doubt this is the opening night.
And whatever I'll do
will turn for ever into what I've done.

Theatrical impressions

In tragedy I find the sixth act most important:
when they arise from stage battlefields,
adjust their wigs and robes,
pull out the knife from the breast,
remove the noose from the neck,
stand in line amongst the living
facing the audience.

Bows individual and collective:
a white hand on a wounded heart,
a suicide curtseying,
a beheaded nodding.

Bows in pairs:
fury offering an arm to gentleness,
the victim gazing blissfully into the torturer's eyes,
the revolutionary ungrudgingly marching with the tyrant.

Eternity squashed with the toe of a golden slipper.
Morals dispersed with the brim of a hat.
An incorrigible readiness to repeat it all tomorrow.

A file of those who died much earlier
in acts three and four and between the acts.
The miraculous return of those vanished without trace.

The thought that in the wings they patiently waited
not shedding their costumes
not taking off their make-up
moves me more than tragic tirades.

But truly uplifting is the falling curtain
and what can still be glimpsed beneath it:
here a hand hastily grabs a flower,
there another snatches a dropped sword.
Only then a third, unseen,
accomplishes its task:
grips me by the throat.

Water

The drop of water on my hand
is drawn from the Ganges and the Nile,

from the sky-ascending hoar on a seal's whisker,
from broken jars in the cities of Ys and Tyre.

On my index-finger
the Caspian Sea is an open sea

and the Pacific meekly drains into the Rudawa,
the very river that sailed in a cloud over Paris

in the year seventeen-hundred-and-sixty-four
on the seventh of May at three in the morning.

There aren't enough lips to utter
your fleeting names, Oh water!

I would need to name you in every tongue,
voicing together every single vowel

and simultaneously keep mum — for the benefit
of the lake still awaiting a name,

with no place on earth — and for
the heavenly star reflected in it.

Someone's been drowning, someone dying has been calling
you.
That was long ago and happened yesterday.

You've dowsed homes, you've snatched them
like trees, snatched forests like cities.

You were present in baptismal fonts and courtesans' baths.
In kisses, in shrouds.

Biting stones, feeding rainbows.
In the sweat and dew of pyramids and lilacs.

How light a drop of rain.
How gently the world touches me.

Wherever, whenever, whatever took place
is recorded on the waters of babel.

The sky

That's where one should have started: the sky.
A window without a sill, without frames or panes.
An opening, and nothing besides,
but gaping wide.

I needn't wait for a clear night
nor crane my neck
to examine the sky.
The sky is behind me, under my hand, on my eye-lids.
The sky wraps me up tightly
and lifts me from below.

Even the highest mountains
are not nearer the sky
than deepest valleys.
At no point is there more of it
than at another.
A cloud is crushed by the sky
as ruthlessly as a grave.
A mole as sky-ascending
as a wing-flapping owl.
An object falling into an abyss
falls from the sky to sky.

Granular, fluid, rocky,
fiery and airborne
expanses of sky, crumbs of sky,
gusts and snatches of sky.
The sky ever-present
even in darkness beneath the skin.

I eat sky, I defecate sky.
I am a trap inside a trap.
A dwelt-in dweller,
an embraced embrace,
a question in answer to a question.

The division into sky and earth
is not a proper way
of considering this whole.
It only allows one
to survive under a more precise address,
quicker to find,
should any one seek me.
My distinguishing marks
are wonder and despair.

Railway station

My non-arrival in M
was strictly on time.

I warned you
with my unposted letter.

You managed not to meet me
at the expected hour.

The train pulled-in at platform 3.
Lots of people got out.

My absence joined the crowd
at the exit.

Two or three women
rushed to stand in for me
in that rush.

Someone I didn't recognise
ran up to one of them,
but she recognised him
at once.

The two exchanged
a kiss which wasn't ours,
and a suitcase which wasn't mine
got lost.

The railway station in M
achieved excellent grades
for objective existence.

Everything was in its place.
Particulars moved
along designated rails.

Even the arranged meeting
occurred.

Beyond the range
of our presence.

In paradise lost
of probability.

Somewhere else.
Somewhere else.
How these tiny words reverberate.

May be left untitled

It's come to pass that one sunny morning
I am sitting under a tree
on a river-bank.
It's a trivial event
history will not record.
It's not like wars or treaties
whose causes await scrutiny
nor memorable assassinations of tyrants.

And yet I am sitting on a river-bank, that's a fact.
And since I am here,
I must have come from somewhere,
and earlier
I must have been around many places,
just like conquerors of kingdoms
before they set sail.

The fleeting moment also has its past,
its Friday before Saturday,
May preceeding June.
Its horizons are as real
as they are in commanders' field-glasses.

This tree — a poplar with ancient roots.
The river is the Raba: flowing since beyond yesterday.
The path through the thickets: made not the day before.
To blow away the clouds
the wind must first have blown them here.
And though nothing significant is happening nearby,
the world is not therefore the poorer in details,
the less justified, less well defined
then when it was being conquered by nomadic people.

Silence is not confined to secret plots,
the pageant of causes to coronations.
Pebbles by-passed on the beach can be as rounded
as the anniversaries of insurrections.

The embroidery of circumstance is also twisty and thick.
The ant's seam in the grass.
The grass sewn into the earth.
The pattern of a wave darned by a stick.

It just so happens I am and I look.
Nearby a white butterfly flutters in the air
with wings that are wholly his
and the shadow that flies over my hands
is not other, not anyone's, but his very own.

Seeing such sights I lose my certainty
that what is important
is more important than the unimportant.

Reality demands

Reality demands
that this too should be known:
life goes on.
It does at Cannae and at Borodino
on Kosovo Field and Guernica.

There is a petrol station
in a small square in Jericho,
there are freshly painted seats
at Bila Hora.*
Letters are sent
from Pearl Harbour to Hastings, a removals-van passes
watched by the lion of Cheronea,
while a weather-front
inescapably moves towards
the blossoming orchards near Verdun.

There is so much of Everything
that Nothing is quite efficiently veiled.
Music flows
from yachts at Actium
and couples are dancing on decks in sunlight.

So much keeps happening
that it must be happening everywhere,
wherever stone is piled on stone
there an ice-cream van

---

* Site near Prague of a battle during the Thirty Years' War (*Transl.*)

58

besieged by kids;
wherever Hieroshima,
there Hieroshima again
and the manufacture of many objects
for daily consumption.

It's not without attractions, this terrible world,
not without dawns
for which waking is worthwhile.
In the fields of Maciejowice**
grass is green
and in it, as you would expect,
transparent dew.

Perhaps all sights have been battlefields,
those still remembered,
those already forgotten,
forests of birches, cedars, firs, white snows,
yellow sands, grey gravel, opalescent bogs
and ravines full of defeats
where in sudden need
you can crouch under a bush.

What moral flows from this — none, probably.
What really flows — fast-congealing blood
and always some river or other, some clouds.
In tragic mountain-passes
the wind snatches hats
and there is little you can do about it —
the sight is amusing.

** Site in Poland of a battle in 1794 between Poles and Russians. (*Transl.*)

The classic

A few clods of earth and the life will be forgotten.
The music will be freed of circumstance.
No more of the maestro's coughs when the minuets are
                                                    played.
The poultices will be torn away.
A fire will consume the wig full of dust and lice.
Ink-stains will vanish from ruffles.
Shoes, the uncomfortable witnesses, will be dumped.
The least-gifted pupil will inherit the violin.
Butcher's bills will be removed from the scores.
The wretched mother's letters will end up in the bellies of
                                                    mice.
The quashed ill-starred romance will be obliterated.
Eyes will not fill with tears.
The neighbours' daughter will find a use for the pink ribbon.
The times, God be praised, are not Romantic yet.
Whatever is not a quartet
will fifth-like be rejected.
Whatever is not a quintet,
will sixth-like be snuffed-out.
Whatever is not the choir of forty angels,
will fall silent like a squealing dog or a hiccoughing
                                                    policeman.
The vase of aloe, the saucer with fly-poison
and the jar of pomade will be cleared from the window,
revealing — but of course! — a view
of the garden never seen before.
And now listen, Oh listen, ye mortals,
attentively prick your astonished ears,
Oh attentive, Oh astonished, Oh listening mortals,
listen — Oh listeners — all ears now!

Letters of the dead

We read the letters of the dead like helpless gods,
yet gods nevertheless knowing later dates.
We know which debts were never settled,
whom the widows hastily married.
Poor dead, blinded dead,
deceived, error-prone, awkwardly provident.
We see the faces and gestures made behind their backs.
Our ears catch the rustle of wills torn to shreds.
They sit before us like ridiculous gnomes
or chase their hats the wind had snatched.
Their bad taste, Napoleon, steam and electricity,
their deadly cures for curable illnesses,
the foolish Apocalypse according to St John,
the false paradise on earth according to Jean-Jacques...
We watch in silence their pawns on the chess-board
now moved merely three squares further on.
Everything they foretold has turned out quite differently,
or somewhat differently, that is, again, quite differently.
The most earnest ones look trustingly into our eyes
because according to their calculations they would see
perfection.

A version of events

If they did let us choose,
we probably pondered long.

The proposed bodies were uncomfortable
and wore out hideously.

Ways of
satisfying hunger disgusted us,
we were repelled
by will-lessly inherited characteristics
and the tyranny of glands.

The world that was to surround us
was steadily falling apart.
There was a free-for-all for effects of causes.
The majority of specific fates
we were offered for scrutiny
we rejected
with sadness and horror.

Questions like the following came up:
is it worth
bearing in pain a dead child
and why be a sailor
who will not reach land.

We consented to death,
but not in every form.
We were drawn to love,
fine, but love
that kept its promises.

We were frightened off
both by the fragility of value-judgments
and the impermanence of masterpieces.

All wished for a country
without neighbours
and a life
between the wars.

None of us wished to rule
or be ruled,
no one wished to be a victim
of his own or others' illusions,
there were no volunteers
for crowds and processions,
and even less desire to join decaying tribes
— but without these history
could not roll
through expected epochs.

Meanwhile a large number
of shining stars
had already gone dark and cold.
Now was the time to decide.

At last, insisting on numerous conditions,
applicants emerged for posts of explorers and healers,
for one or two unsung philosophers,
for a couple of nameless gardeners,
conjurers and musicians
— though due to shortage of candidates
even those lives
remained unfulfilled.

The whole business
needed to be reconsidered.

Weren't we offered a journey
from which we would return
assuredly and swiftly?

A sojourn beyond eternity
quite monotonous after all
and knowing no movement
might never have been repeated.

We began to doubt
whether knowing all in advance
we really knew everything.

Whether a choice so premature
is a choice at all.
Whether it would be better
to forget it,
or if choose
— then choose *there*.

We have observed the earth.
Certain dare-devils were there already.

A weak plant
clutched at a rock
with a frivolous trust
that the wind would not uproot her.

A smallish animal
was digging itself out of a hole
with a determination and hope we found puzzling.

We seemed to ourselves too cautious,
mean-minded and ridiculous.

Anyway, our numbers were dwindling.
Those most impatient had disappeared somewhere.
They were first into the fire
— yes, that was clear.
They were just starting it
on a steep bank of a real river.

Some
were even returning.
But not in our direction.
And they seemed to be carrying a trophy.

Unwritten poem reviewed

In the opening words of her composition
the author asserts that the Earth is small,
while the sky in unconscionably vast
and, I quote, "contains more than necessary" stars.

In her description of the heavens one detects a certain
                                                    helplessness,
the author loses herself in the terrible void,
she is struck by the lifelessness of many planets
and presently her mind (which lacks rigour)
poses the question
whether, after all, we are alone
under the sun, under all the suns of the universe.

Flouting the calculus of probability!
And all the generally accepted convictions!
Despite incontrovertible proof which any day now
may fall into our hands! Ah, well, poetry.

Meanwhile, our oracle returns to Earth,
a planet which perhaps "rolls on without witness",
the sole "science-fiction cosmos can afford".
The despair of Pascal (1623–1662 [Ed.])
appears to the author to have no match
on Andromeda or Cassiopeia.
Uniqueness exaggerates and obligates,
and thus arises the problem of how to live, and so on,
since "emptiness will not resolve that for us".
"My God, man cries to His Own Self,
have mercy on me, bring me light..."

The author is haunted by the thought of life so effortlessly
fritted away,
as though there were endless supplies of it;
by wars which — according to her perverse opinion —
are always lost on both sides;
by man's "policification" (*sic!*) of man.
A moral intent flickers in the work
and would probably have glowed under a less naïve pen.

A pity, though. This fundamentally risky thesis
(are we, after all, perhaps alone
beneath the sun, beneath all the suns of the universe)
and its development in her happy-go-lucky style
(a mixture of loftiness and common speech)
causes us to ask whether anyone would believe it.
No one surely. Quite so.

Rachunek elegijny

Ilu tych, których znałam,
jeśli naprawdę ich znałam,
mężczyzn, kobiet,
jeśli ten podział pozostaje w mocy,
przestąpiło ten próg,
jeśli próg,
przebiegło przez ten most,
jeśli nazwać to mostem -

Ilu po życiu krótszym albo dłuższym,
jeśli to dla nich wciąż jakaś różnica,
dobrym, bo się zaczęło,
złym, bo się skończyło,
jeśliby nie woleli powiedzieć na odwrót,
znalazło się na drugim brzegu,
jeśli znalazło się
a drugi brzeg istnieje —

Nie dana mi jest pewność
ich dalszego losu,
jeśli to nawet jeden wspólny los
i jeszcze los —

Wszystko,
jeśli słowem tym nie ograniczam,
mają za sobą,
jeśli nie przed sobą

An elegiac account

How many of those I've known,
if truly I knew them,
men, women,
if this division remains in force,
have crossed the threshold,
have run across this bridge,
if it is a bridge —

How many after a briefer or longer life,
if that still represents a distinction for them,
good, because it had begun,
bad, because it's concluded,
if they didn't wish to say the opposite,
have found themselves on the other shore,
if they have found themselves
and the other shore exists —

I have not been granted certitude
regarding their further fate,
if it's really one single fate
and fate still —

Everything,
if that word doesn't delimit,
they have behind them,
if not before them —

Ilu ich wyskoczyło z pędzącego czasu
i w oddaleniu coraz rzewniej znika,
jeśli warto wierzyć perspektywie —
Ilu, jeżeli pytanie ma sens,
jeżeli można dojść do sumy ostatecznej
zanim liczący nie doliczy siebie,
zapadło w ten najgłębszy sen,
jeśli nie ma głębszego —

Do widzenia.
Do jutra.
Do następnego spotkania.
Już tego nie chcą,
jeżeli nie chcą, powtórzyć.
Zdani na nieskończone,
jeśli nie inne, milczenie.
Zajęci tylko tym,
jeżeli tylko tym,
do czego ich przymusza nieobecność.

How many have jumped off the speeding time
and are disappearing into mounting melancholy
if perspective's to be believed —
how many, if the question makes sense,
if one can reach the final sum
before he who counts includes himself,
have fallen into this deepest sleep,
if there is no deeper —

Good-bye.
See you tomorrow.
Until next time.
Now they don't wish,
if they don't, to repeat this.
Condemned in infinite,
if no other, silence.
Absorbed only in that,
if only that,
to which absence constrains them.

Index of titles

Other Titles from
FOREST BOOKS

International Poetry Series

AN ANTHOLOGY OF CONTEMPORARY ROMANIAN POETRY
Translated by Andrea Deletant and Brenda Walker.
0 9509487 4 8 paper £6.95   112 pages

ANTHOLOGY OF SORBIAN POETRY 1550–1990
Translated from the *Sorbian* by Robert Elsie.
UNESCO collection of representative works.
0 948259 72 8 papier £6.95   176 pages

ARIADNE'S THREAD An anthology of contemporary Polish women
poets. Translated from the *Polish* by Susan Bassnett and Piotr
Kuhiwczak. UNESCO collection of representative works.
0 948259 45 0 paper £6.95   96 pages

BEFORE WE WERE STRANGES Poems by the *American* poet Nadya
Aisenberg. Introduced by Sylvia Kantaris.
0 948259 81 7 paper £6.95   96 pages

CALL YOURSELF ALIVE? The love poems of Nina Cassian. Translated
from the *Romanian* by Andrea Deletant and Brenda Walker.
Introduction by Fleur Adcock.
0 948259 38 8 paper £6.95   96 pages   Illustrated

CLOSED CIRCUIT by Shadab Vajdi.
Translated from the *Persian* by Lotfali Kohonji
and introduced by Peter Avery.
0 948259 78 7 paper £6.95   96 pages

CONTEMPORARY POETRY FROM THE CANARY ISLANDS
Translated by Louis Bourne. Dual text English/Spanish.
0 948259 73 6 paper £9.95   224 pages

ENCHANTING BEASTS An anthology of Finnish women poets.
Translated from the *Finnish* and the *Swedish* by Kirsti Simonsuuri.
0 948259 68 X paper £8.95   160 pages

THE EYE IN THE MIRROR Selected poems of Takis Varvitsiotis.
Translated from the *Greek* by Kimon Friar. (Forest/Paratiritis)
0 948259 59 0 paper £8.95   160 pages

EXILE ON A PEPPERCORN Selected poems by Mircea Dinescu.
Translated from the *Romanian* by Andrea Deletant
and Brenda Walker.
0 948259 00 0 paper £7.95   96 pages   Illustrated

FIRES OF THE SUNFLOWER Selected poems by Ivan Davidkov.
Translated from the *Bulgarian* by Ewald Osers.
0 948259 48 5 paper £6.95   96 pages   Illustrated

FISH RINGS ON WATER Selected poems by Katherine Gallagher,
the *Australian* poet. Introduced by Peter Porter.
0 948259 75 2 paper £6.95   96 pages   Illustrated

FOOTPRINTS OF THE WIND Selected poems of Mateja Matevski.
Translated from the *Macedonian* by Ewald Osers.
Introduction by Robin Skelton.
0 948259 41 8 paper £6.95   96 pages   Illustrated

THE ROAD TO FREEDOM Poems by Geo Milev
Translated from the *Bulgarian* by Ewald Osers

UNESCO collection of representative works.
0 948259 40 X paper £6.95   96 pages   Illustrated

ROOM WITHOUT WALLS Selected poems of Bo Carpelan.
Translated from the *Swedish* by Anne Born.
0 948259 08 6 paper £7.95   144 pages   Illustrated

SILENT VOICES An anthology of contemporary Romanian women
poets. Translated by Andrea Deletant and Brenda Walker.
Introduced by Fleur Adcock.
0 948259 03 5 paper £8.95   172 pages

SNOW AND SUMMERS Selected poems of Solveig von Schoultz.
Translated from *Finland/Swedish* by Anne Born. Introduction by
Bo Carpelan.
0 948259 52 3 paper £7.95   112 pages

SPRING TIDE Selected poems of Pia Tafdrup.
Translated from the *Danish* by Anne Born.
0 948259 55 8 paper £7.95   96 pages

STEP HUMAN INTO THIS WORLD Poems by Olaf Munzberg.
Translated from the *German* by Mitch Cohen.
0 948259 53 1 paper £6.95   96 pages

STOLEN FIRE Selected poems by Lyubomir Levchev.
Translated from the *Bulgarian* by Ewald Osers. Introduction
by John Balaban.

UNESCO collection of representative works.
0 948259 04 3 paper £6.95   112 pages   Illustrated

THROUGH THE NEEDLE'S EYE Selected poems of Jon Milos.
Translated from the *Romanian* by Brenda Walker and Jon Milos.
0 948259 61 2 paper £6.95   96 pages   Illustrated

THE TRAPPED STRAWBERRY Poems by Petru Cărdu.
Translated from the *Romanian* by Brenda Walker with Dušica
Marinkov. Introduction by Daniel Weissbort.
0 948259 83 3 paper £6.95   96 pages

THE TWELFTH MAN Poems by Iftikhar Arif.
Translated from the *Urdu* by Brenda Walker. Dual text.
0 948259 49 3 paper £6.95   96 pages

A VANISHING EMPTINESS Selected poems of Willem M. Roggeman.
Edited by Yann Lovelock. Translated from the *Dutch*.
0 948259 51 5 £7.95   112 pages   Illustrated

WASTELANDS OF FIRE Poems by Ku Sang.
Translated from the *Korean* by Anthony Teague.
0 948259 82 5 paper £7.95   144 pages

THE WORLD AS IF Selected poems of Uffe Harder.
Translated from the *Danish* by John F. Deane and Uffe Harder.
(Dedalus/Forest)
0 948259 76 0 paper £4.95   80 pages

YOUNG POETS FROM A NEW BULGARIA
Edited by Belin Tonchev.
0 948259 71 X paper £7.95   162 pages

GATES OF THE MOMENT Selected poems of Ion Stoica.
Translated from the *Romanian* by Brenda Walker and Andrea
Deletant. Dual text with cassette.
0 9509487 0 5 paper £6.95   126 pages   Cassette £3.50 plus VAT

IN CELEBRATION OF MIHAI EMINESCU Selected poems and extracts
translated from the *Romanian* by Brenda Walker and Horia Florian
Popescu. Illustrated by Sabin Balaşa.
0 948259 62 0 cloth £20   176 pages

JOUSTS OF APHRODITE Poems collected from the Greek Anthology
Book V
Translated from the *Greek* into modern English by Michael Kelly.
0 948259 05 1 cloth £6.95   0 948259 34 5 paper £4.95   96 pages

LAND AND PEACE Selected poems of Desmond Egan.
Translated *into Irish* by Michael Hartnett, Gabriel Rosenstock,
Douglas Sealey and Tomas MacSiomoin. Dual text.
0 948259 64 7 paper £7.95   112 pages

LET'S TALK ABOUT THE WEATHER Selected poems of Marin Sorescu
Translated from the *Romanian* by Andrea Deletant and Brenda
Walker. Introduction by Jon Silkin.
0 9509487 8 0 paper £6.95   96 pages

YOUNG POETS FROM A NEW ROMANIA
Translated by Brenda Walker and Andrea Deletant.
0 948259 89 2 paper £8.95   176 pages

LOVE SONNETS OF THE RENAISSANCE
Translated from the *French, Italian* and *Spanish* and *Portuguese*
by Laurence Kitchin.
0 948259 60 4 paper £6.95   96 pages   Dual text

THE NAKED MACHINE Selected poems of Matthías Johannessen.
Translated from the *Icelandic* by Marshall Brement. (Forest/Almenna
bokáfélagid)
0 948259 44 2 cloth £7.95   0 948259 43 4 paper £5.95   96
pages   Illustrated

ON THE CUTTING EDGE Selected poems of Justo Jorge Padrón.
Translated from the *Spanish* by Louis Bourne.
0 948259 42 6 paper £8.95   176 pages

PEOPLE ON A BRIDGE Poems by Wislawa Szymborska.
Translated from the *Polish* by Adam Czerniawski.
0 948259 70 1 paper £6.95   96 pages

PIED POETS An anthology of Romanian Transylvanian and Danube
poets writing in German. Translated from the *German* by Robert
Elsie. Dual text English/German.
0 948259 77 9 paper £6.95   208 pages

POETS OF BULGARIA An anthology of contemporary Bulgarian poets.
Edited by William Meredith. Introduction by Alan Brownjohn.
0 948259 39 6 paper £6.95   112 pages

PORTRAIT OF THE ARTIST AS AN ABOMINABLE SNOWMAN
Selected poems of Gabriel Rosenstock translated from the *Irish*
by Michael Hartnett. New Poems translated by Jason Sommer.
0 948259 56 6 paper £7.95   112 pages   Dual text

International Drama Series

THE HOUR OF THE LYNX A play by Per Olov Enquist.
Translated from the *Swedish* by Ross Shideler.
0 948259 85 X paper £6.95   64 pages

THE THIRST OF THE SALT MOUNTAIN Three plays by Marin Sorescu
Jonah, The Verger, and the Matrix) Translated from the *Romanian*
by Andrea Deletant and Brenda Walker.
0 9509487 5 6 paper £7.95   124 pages   Illustrated

VLAD DRACULA THE IMPALER A play by Marin Sorescu
Translated from the *Romanian* by Dennis Deletant.
0 948259 07 8 paper £6.95   112 pages   Illustrated

International Short Story Series

DUBAI TALES by Muhammad al Murr.
Translated from the *Arabic* by Peter Clark.
0 948259 86 8 paper £8.95   176 pages

FANTASTIC TALES by Mircea Eliade and Mihai Niculescu.
Translated from the *Romanian* by Eric Tappe.
0 948259 92 2 paper £7.95   112 pages

HEARTWORK Stories of Solveig von Schoultz.
Translated from *Finland/Swedish* by Marlaine Delargy
and Joan Tate. Introduction by Bo Carpelan.
0 948259 50 7 paper £7.95   144 pages

PREPARATIONS FOR FLIGHT and other Swedish stories.
Translated from the *Swedish* by Robin Fulton.
0 948259 66 3 paper £8.95   176 pages

RUNNING TO THE SHROUDS Six sea stories
of Konstantin Stanyukovich.
Translated from the *Russian* by Neil Parsons.
0 948259 06 X paper £6.95   112 pages

THE SEER AND OTHER STORIES by Jonas Lie.
Translated from the *Norwegian* by Brian Morton and Richard
Trevor.
0 948259 65 5 paper £8.95   160 pages

THE TALISMAN Stories and poems by Ganga Prasad Vimal.
Edited by Wendy Wright.
0 948259 57 4 paper £9.95   208 pages   Dual text English/Hindi.

THICKHEAD AND OTHER STORIES by Haldun Taner.
Translated from the *Turkish* by Geoffrey Lewis.
UNESCO collection of representative works.
0 948259 58 2 paper £8.95   160 pages

A WOMAN'S HEART Stories by Jordan Yovkov.
Translated from the *Bulgarian* by John Burnip.
0 948259 54 X paper £9.95   208 pages

YOUTH WITHOUT YOUTH and other Novellas by Mircea Eliade.
Edited and with an introduction by Matei Calinescu.
Translated from the *Romanian* by MacLinscott Ricketts.
0 948259 74 4 paper £12.95   328 pages

FOREST BOOKS

DRUKARNIA NARODOWA W KRAKOWIE